Zorgen voor mijn ballon.

Een praktische vertaling van de window of tolerance voor kinderen.

Eleonora Tilkin-Franssens

ISBN: 9798359825443

De window of tolerance is een theorie die gecreëerd werd door Dr. Dan Siegel.

Voor mijn miniteam blauw dat altijd klaarstaat om constructieve feedback te geven als ik iets op papier probeer te zetten.

Dit is een ballon.
Als ik deze ballon goed opblaas – niet te hard en
niet te zacht – en ik leg er een knoopje in, dan
kan ik ermee: gooien, laten botsen, aan een
slinger hangen en nog zoveel meer.

Als alle lucht uit mijn ballon loopt, dan is mijn
ballon plat.
Dan kan ik er niet zoveel meer mee doen.

Gelukkig kan ik mijn ballon wel weer opblazen.

Als ik mijn ballon te hard opblaas en die heel
hard wordt dan zou die kunnen ontploffen.
Als mijn ballon ontploft, kan ik er niets meer
mee doen.

Gelukkig kan ik er als ik er op let op tijd wat
lucht uitlaten.

WAT?
WIE?
WAAR?
WANNEER?
HOE?

Ons hoofd werkt ook zo'n beetje als een ballon.
Als alles goed gaat, we weten wat we kunnen
doen en wat er van ons verwacht wordt… dan
gaat alles precies vanzelf.
We kunnen goed naar onze leerkracht luisteren,
we kunnen fijn samenspelen, ons werk maken
lukt goed, we kunnen ons focussen.
Op dat moment is onze ballon net goed
opgeblazen.
Er zit niet teveel lucht in en ook niet te weinig
lucht.

Goed slapen, gezond eten en drinken, vrienden
hebben, begrepen worden, leuke dingen doen en
begrijpen wat de opdracht is, helpt om te zorgen
dat onze ballon goed opgeblazen is en niet te
snel leegloopt en ook niet te snel vol raakt.

Wat helpt jou om je goed te voelen zodat alles
vanzelf lijkt te gaan?

Hoe merk je aan jezelf dat je ballon goed
opgeblazen is?

Sommige dingen kunnen ervoor zorgen dat onze
ballon leegloopt of zo hard wordt opgeblazen
dat hij bijna ontploft.
Dat kunnen dingen zijn zoals te veel werk
hebben, de opdracht niet begrijpen, iemand die
tegen je roept of je pijn doet, te veel rommel om
je heen, elkaar niet begrijpen, niet weten wat je
moet doen…

Wat zijn dingen die er bij jou voor zorgen dat je
ballon leegloopt of te hard wordt opgeblazen?

Als er heel veel om je heen gebeurt dat je niet
begrijpt en je denkt dat je het niet kan, dan kan
het gebeuren dat je ineens niets meer kan. Dat je
niet meer kan opletten, niet meer kan luisteren
en je gewoon afstaat.
Dan ben je precies een leeggelopen ballon.

Hebben je dat al eens meegemaakt?

Hoe merk je aan jezelf dat je ballon leeggelopen
is?

STOP

Of het kan gebeuren dat het je niet meer lukt om
stil te zitten, dat je begint te roepen of dat je
iemand pijn doet of iets stuk doet. Dan lijkt het
of je niet meer kan stoppen en het niet kan
tegenhouden.
Dan ben je precies een ballon die te hard wordt
opgeblazen en (bijna) ontploft.

Gebeurt dat soms bij jou?

Hoe merk je aan jezelf dat je ballon gaat
ontploffen?

Niet iedereen zijn ballon is even groot.
Als je een grote ballon hebt, dan kan daar veel
lucht in zonder dat die ontploft en duurt het ook
heel lang voor je ballon leegloopt.
Als je een kleine ballon hebt, dan kan daar niet
zo veel lucht in zonder dat die ontploft en kan je
ballon snel leeglopen.

Het kan ook zijn dat je tijdens het spelen een
grote ballon hebt en tijdens het rekenen een
kleine ballon.
Of dat je op school een kleine ballon hebt en
thuis een grote ballon.

Waar heb jij een kleine ballon en waar heb je een
grote ballon?

Bij wie heb je een grote ballon en bij wie heb je
een kleine ballon?

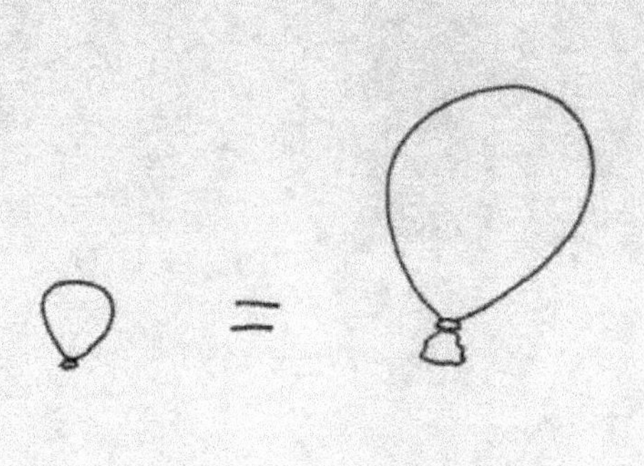

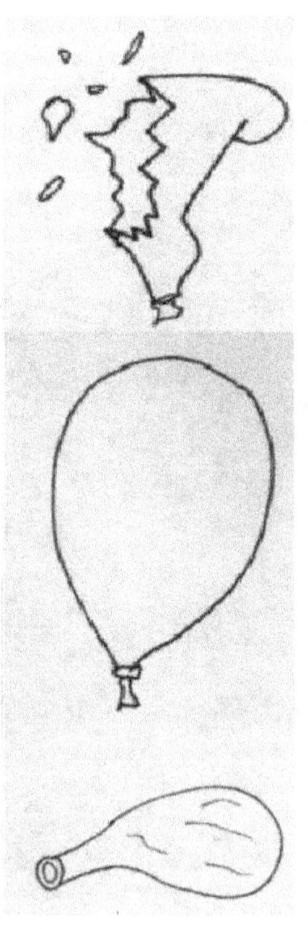

Gelukkig kan je oefenen om een grotere ballon te krijgen zodat je het makkelijker vindt om mee te doen en een fijne dag te hebben.

Wanneer merken jullie dat jullie ballon goed is opgeblazen zonder dat die leeg loopt of ontploft?

Wanneer merken jullie dat jullie ballon aan het leeglopen is of op ontploffen staat?

Dingen zoals diep ademhalen, even een frisse
neus halen, iets drinken, uitleg vragen… kunnen
je helpen om je ballon wat meer op te blazen of
een beetje leeg te laten lopen.

Wat hebben jullie al ontdekt dat helpt?

Wat kan je zelf doen?

Wat kan iemand anders doen?

Mijn ballon werkt zo.

Mijn ballon is goed opgeblazen …
(teken of schrijf)

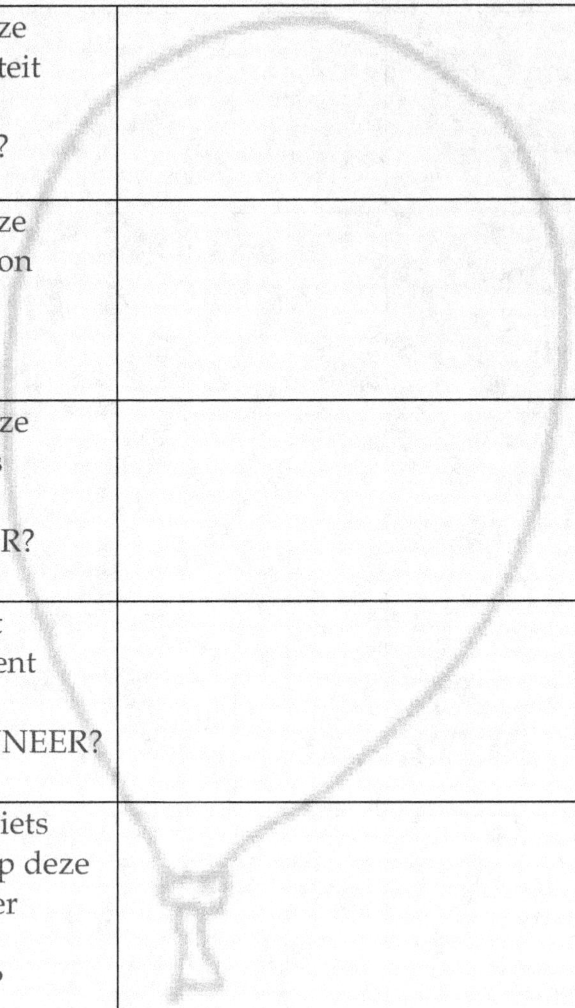

bij deze activiteit WAT?	
bij deze persoon WIE?	
op deze plaats WAAR?	
op dit moment WANNEER?	
als ik iets doe op deze manier HOE?	

Mijn ballon loopt leeg…
(teken of schrijf)

bij deze activiteit WAT?	
bij deze persoon WIE?	
op deze plaats WAAR?	
op dit moment WANNEER?	
als ik iets doe op deze manier HOE?	

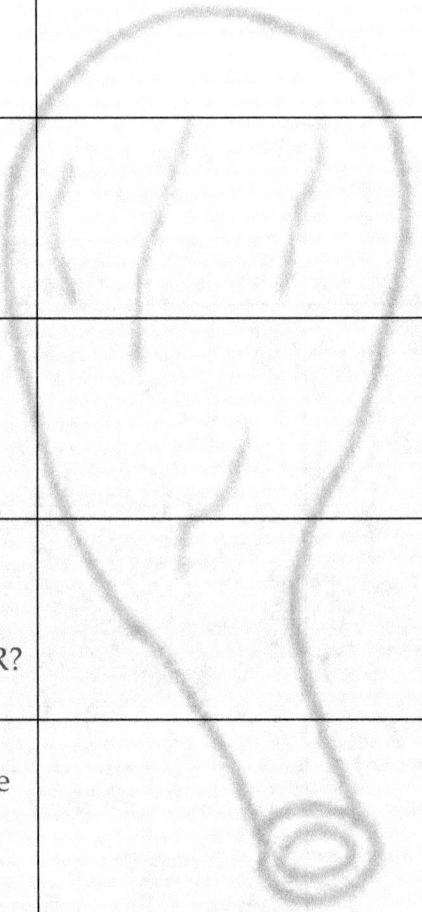

Mijn ballon ontploft (bijna) …
(teken of schrijf)

bij deze activiteit WAT?	
bij deze persoon WIE?	
op deze plaats WAAR?	
op dit moment WANNEER?	
als ik iets doe op deze manier HOE?	

Zo zorg ik voor mijn ballon.

Ik kan mijn ballon een beetje laten leeglopen als
…
(teken of schrijf)

ik dit doe	
ik naar deze persoon ga	
als ik hier naartoe ga	
als iemand anders mij op deze manier helpt	

Ik kan mijn ballon een beetje opblazen als …
(teken of schrijf)

ik dit doe	
ik naar deze persoon ga	
als ik hier naartoe ga	
als iemand anders mij op deze manier helpt	

Nawoord voor ouders

In de Window of tolerance beschrijft dr. Dan Siegel het raam – in dit geval de ballon – als de optimale staat van alertheid. Als je in je raam bent, kan je goed meedoen en reageer je adequaat op stress en op alles wat er op je pad komt.

Ga je uit je raam – door teveel triggers, post-traumatische stress, overprikkeling… - en verhoogt je staat van alertheid zo hard dat je uit je raam gaat en je lichaam dus in overlevingsmodus gaat, dan kunnen er twee dingen gebeuren.

Of je gaat in bevries-modus en verstijft, waardoor je in hypo-alertheid gaat. Je komt futloos over, je reageert traag…

Of je gaat in vecht-vlucht-modus en dan kan het zijn dat je roept, anderen pijn doet, wegloopt…

Je kiest zelf niet of je alertheid verhoogt en je uit je raam gaat. Het is een automatische reactie van je hersenen op het gepercipieerde gevaar.

Via dit boekje leren kinderen zichzelf beter kennen en zichzelf te hanteren. Daarnaast helpt het eveneens om samen met je kind op zoek te gaan naar wat de volwassenen kunnen doen om het kind te helpen zich beter te reguleren en dus meer aanwezig te zijn.

Echt aanwezig kunnen zijn in een situatie, zonder stress, zorgt ervoor dat kinderen tot leren kunnen komen. Veel succes in jullie gezamenlijk zoektocht!

Over de auteur

Eleonora heeft zowel professionele als persoonlijke ervaring met dit onderwerp, zowel van de binnenkant als de buitenkant.

Ze heeft een bachelor in onderwijs, zorgverbreding & remediërend leren, autisme en toegepaste psychologie en werkt al meer dan 10 jaar in de onderwijscontext.

Ze gebruikt de ballon om kinderen te helpen zich bewuster te worden van hun eigen noden en hoe ze deze kunnen vervullen en om zorgfiguren te ondersteunen in het beter begrijpen van kinderen wiens ballon te snel leeg of overvol is.

www.ingramcontent.com/pod-product-compliance
Lightning Source LLC
Chambersburg PA
CBHW051720250726
48653CB00008B/3120

Grooming is essential, not only for removing dead hair from the thick coat but also for maintaining the cleanliness of the face wrinkles. A speedy daily grooming session, even just a swipe with a hound mitt, is typically sufficient for the coat, and a delicate wiping with a moist towel is all that is required to maintain the face.

History Despite the fact that the pug is often linked with Holland, the breed really originated in China. It is believed that the pug was bred down from a local mastiff-type dog. Following this step, the small dogs with the round heads and wrinkled faces were brought to Holland by commercial ships owned by the Dutch East India Company. It was in 1572 that a pug sounded the alarm that rescued Prince William from the oncoming Spanish army, and the breed has since been inextricably linked to the House of Orange, which is the royal family of Orange.

The duke and duchess of Windsor also kept a pug as a royal companion throughout their time in Windsor, as did the wife of Napoleon. The pug became the most popular breed of dog in Victorian England, and you can see quite a few depictions of the breed in artworks from that time period.

The name "pug" may have originated from the Latin word "pugnus," which means "fist," and may have been used to describe the spherical face and head. The nature of the breed does not correspond to the name of the breed at all since these dogs were not intended to be guard dogs but rather companion dogs first and foremost.

Pugs are well-known for their adorable appearance, which includes their round, squishy faces. This breed is perfect for laid-back families and those who like doting on their pets since it may be naughty at times but is adored by the people who own it. However, pugs are susceptible to many of the same health problems as other dogs. Here is the information you need in order to live with pugs and properly care for them.

Appearance of a Pug Temperament Living Needs Care The Medical Record Fun Facts

Height: 10 to 13 inches Weight: 14 to 18 pounds Lifespan: 13 to 15 years Breed Size: Pug Height: 10 to 13 inches Weight: 14 to 18 pounds

• small (0-25 lbs.)

excellent with children, elderly people, dogs, cats, and families; disposition includes being sociable, outgoing, and playful; intellect includes a high shedding capacity; and regular exercise has to be met.

• low breed group • moderate amount of energy • active level of barking • infrequent quantity of drool • medium level of barking level

• toy coat length and texture
• short colors • fawn • black

patterns • sable other traits • easy to train • easy to groom • prone to health issues • high potential for weight gain • apartment-friendly • good for first-time pet owners • strong loyalty tendencies toy coat length and texture • short colors • fawn • black patterns • sable other traits • easy to train • easy to groom • prone to health issues • high potential for weight gain

Pugs, who were likely originally bred to be lap dogs, thrive on human company and are at their happiest when they are able to be close to their owners. Pugs are known for their crazy antics and rowdy nature, which has earned them the title of "canine class clown."

"They feel that they delight you only by being alive and inhaling your oxygen," says Pam Nichols, DVM, who is set to take over as president of the American Animal Hospital Association in the next year. "They believe that they pleasure you just by being alive."

Because of their calm demeanor and affectionate nature, pugs make wonderful companions within the home. However, you will need to invest in a good vacuum since they shed so much! Pugs are satisfied to do anything their owner wants to do, whether it be watching a movie or going for a stroll around the block. Although they are playful, pugs do not need a significant amount of physical exercise. Pugs are joyful, loving puppies that are highly devoted to their owners. Pugs have a high level of intelligence but may also be stubborn at times.

Pugs are a brachycephalic breed, which means that their lovely smooshed faces may also be the cause of frequent health concerns for the dogs. Prospective pug owners will want to educate themselves on these issues before making the decision to adopt a pug.

Pugs are an old breed with a regal heritage; they have been companions to Chinese emperors, French Empress

Josephine Bonaparte, and Queen Victoria.

Appearance Pugs are characterized by their short muzzles, round faces, and short legs.

According to the American Kennel Club, the average weight of a pug ranges from 14 to 18 pounds, despite the fact that these relatively small dogs pack a lot of muscle onto their square frame. As a result, it is commonly said that the pug's motto is "multum in parvo," which translates to "a lot in a little." The most common colors for pugs are fawn with a black mask or completely black. There are also a few tonal variants within each hue. The hue of the fawn or tan coat may vary from a warm apricot to a chilly and seldom seen silver, depending on the individual animal. Their skulls are characterized by the characteristic short, flat, black snout that is covered with deep wrinkles. Their large, expressive eyes take up much of their wrinkled, goofy face and convey a wide variety of feelings, from surprise and delight to curiosity and even a little bit of fear. They have moles on their cheeks that are often referred to as "beauty spots," and they have a distinct "thumb mark" in the center of their forehead.

They have a short coat, but it is really a double coat, and they shed a lot, particularly during the warmer months of the year. Nichols adds, "I'd call them monster shedders," adding that you should be prepared to have your garments covered with fur and that you should be aware of this possibility. The ideal pug tail, as defined by the standards of the AKC, should have two distinct curls.

Dogs with brachycephalic faces, sometimes known as "smooshed-faced" dogs, such as pugs, confront a few difficulties due to their genetics. Among them include the possibility that their tongues are, quite literally, too big for their mouths, which results in their tongues hanging out of their lips and giving them a perpetually amused expression.

CHAPTER TWO

Temperament:

The best place in the world for a pug to be is right by your side. They have been bred specifically to be companion animals, so they are perfectly satisfied to spend their days lazing about on your lap, dozing off the hours, and even jumping straight into bed with you. However, a word of caution: Because of their wheezing, snorting, and snoring, pug owners may consider purchasing earplugs.

If you do not lavish them with attention or if you leave them alone for extended periods of time, they will become pretty miserable, and they will make sure you are aware of their distress.

It is unrealistic to expect a pug to hunt, protect, or retrieve anything for you. A pug will not participate in such actions under any circumstances. According to the Pug Dog Club of America (PDCA), this does not imply that they aren't up for some romping and playing despite their small stature. Pugs are hilarious little dogs who frequently find their own ways to make their own foolish entertainment; nevertheless, it is important that you pay attention to the show that they are putting on in order to ensure that they are able to preserve their dignity when it is required.

Left: Pugs were bred to be companion animals, and as a result, they like cuddling and spending the day lazing about. They are also tolerant and lively with children, which makes them a favorite among those who are under the age of 18 years old.

Right: Pugs have a tendency to feel apprehensive in response to loud sounds, as well as strange locations and people. Maintain your close proximity to them and convince them that everything is going to be all right!

 Living Needs

Kids adore pugs, and pugs love kids. Although they are

considered to be a toy breed, pugs are sturdier than other dogs of a same size and are eager to engage in play. To save the children any disappointment, explain to them that pugs are not likely to engage in activities such as playing fetch or chasing a soccer ball. Pugs are known for their easygoing nature and ability to get along with a wide variety of companions, including other dogs, cats, rabbits, and even people. Because they don't need a lot of room to move about indoors, pugs are also excellent choices as companion animals for people who live in flats or who are elderly. This makes them a terrific choice. Although this does not necessarily imply that pugs are slothful, it is common knowledge that they may sleep for up to 14 hours every day. They don't bark very often either because to the fact that it might be difficult for them to breathe. Their difficulty breathing, along with the fact that they have small legs, makes them lousy swimmers. Despite this, on very hot summer days, they could probably use a refreshing swim in the pool; they don't handle the heat—or the cold—very well.

Left: Although pugs, like most other dogs, like a good dig in the soil, they are not genetically prone to conduct an excessive amount of digging. Be wary of their muzzles, however: This dirt has the potential to further constrict their already limited nasal airways.

Underbites are common in pugs, just as they are in other brachycephalic breeds such as shih tzus, bulldogs, and French bulldogs. However, you shouldn't assume that this means you have to shell out cash for orthodontic work just yet. Underbites are only addressed if they are causing discomfort or difficulty chewing; the goal of treatment is not to improve the smile's appearance.

Right: The only other coat color that is legally approved

for pugs is black, despite the fact that the most common coat color for pugs is a combination of fawn and black. All-black pugs are exactly what they sound like; their coats will not have any other sign of color in them. (Other from, of course, their hair becoming grayer as they get older)

Care

According to the PDCA's research, your pug may love food even more than they love you, despite the fact that they already adore you. Because of their tiny height, it is possible that they will acquire weight rapidly; as a result, you should be careful to help monitor their intake; restrict the amount of goodies they get, and don't give them table scraps, no matter how adorable and begging their look may be. In addition to that, you should promote exercise, even if kids don't need too much in a day. They come up with ingenious strategies to get rid of their excess energy on their own.

The heavy shedding of a pug may be managed by bathing the dog on a regular basis (approximately once a month) and brushing it often (using a brush with medium-sized bristles, a grooming mitt made of rubber, or a hound glove). Additionally, you need to pay additional care to those cute wrinkles on your face since, if they are filthy and wet, they may become a breeding ground for illness. After giving your pug a bath, be sure to pat it dry completely, and use a dry cotton ball to remove any wrinkles that may have formed in the meantime. In addition, pugs require frequent nail trimming since their nails do not break down naturally from spending a lot of time outside as other breeds do. Because pugs are prone to developing gum disease, it is imperative that their teeth be brushed on a consistent basis.

Training might be difficult at times. These children are more challenging to instruct, and they are not very interested in hearing your point of view. Because of how readily their emotions may be harmed, harsh training approaches should be avoided. Keep in mind that their overarching objective is just to spend time with you.

Pugs are known to wheeze, snort, and snore because to the difficulty that they have in breathing due to the compression of their faces. If your pug is going to be sleeping in close proximity to you, you might consider purchasing some ear plugs.

CHAPTER THREE

Health

I warn that pugs had a propensity to rack up significant costs in their first year of life. "They often need nasal resections to have their nostrils enlarged, as well as surgery to have their soft palates shortened. If such operations are not performed, you may anticipate your dog snoring loudly for the rest of its life.

The physiology of pugs makes it difficult for them to breathe, which may lead to snoring, and it also makes it difficult for them to move and stay cool when the temperature is high. These are symptoms of brachycephalic obstructive airway syndrome (BOAS), which may also cause problems with saliva, sleep, and regurgitation. Brachycephalic people are more likely to have this condition.

Pugs are susceptible to a wide variety of other health problems, including as back difficulties, epilepsy, allergies, hemi-vertebrae (also known as malformed vertebrae), hip dysplasia, patellar luxation, and nerve degeneration in later life. Some of these conditions may even manifest in younger pugs. Pugs are susceptible to a wide range of skin disorders, including yeast infections, staph infections, and demodectic mange, amongst others.

Even while their large, black eyes make them seem lovely, they are particularly susceptible to harm. There are a variety of eye conditions that may affect pugs, including corneal ulcers, proptosis, and dry eye. Your family veterinarian is the best person to treat skin issues such as walking dandruff, which is caused by a microscopic mite. Obesity in pugs may make their respiratory difficulties much worse, therefore it is important for pug owners to monitor their pets' weight and ensure they stay at a healthy level.

According to the findings of a research that was published in 2022 and compared the health of pugs to that of other breeds of dogs, pugs have "several significant health-related welfare issues to overcome." According to the findings of the research, pugs had considerably elevated probabilities of BOAS, corneal ulceration, and stenotic nares (which are small nostrils that make it difficult to breathe). In contrast, the researchers found that pugs had a considerably lower adjusted risk of developing cardiac murmurs or lipoma tumors.

Pugs are the only dogs known to be susceptible to the deadly inflammatory brain illness known as Pug Dog Encephalitis. Unfortunately, there is no recognized cause of it, nor is there a test for it. It causes the pug to convulse, spin in circles, get blind, then lapse into a coma, and eventually pass away. The research is still under progress.

Pugs have been around for many centuries and have been depicted in works of art and advertisements for almost as long. During the Victorian period, they were very well-liked and were often depicted on postcards, in paintings, and as figurines in various forms.

History

The pug is a breed of dog that has been around for a very long time and is believed to have originated in China. According to the American

Kennel Club (AKC), around 2,000 years ago, flat-faced or short-nosed toy dogs such as the pug were popular with Chinese emperors and helped them enjoy extravagant lifestyles as a result. Gifts were the sole purpose for which they were used outside of the Far East. But Dutch merchants began arriving in Europe in the 1500s and early 1600s with the breed, and due to the breed's appeal with royal families, it swiftly acquired popularity throughout Europe.

The breed has been known by a variety of names throughout the course of its lengthy history. Some of these names include lo-sze (in Chinese), mopsi (in Finnish), doguillo (in Spanish), and mophonds (in Dutch), amongst others. According to the American Kennel Club (AKC), the term pug is said to have been derived from the Latin word "pugnus," which means "fist," to reflect the fact that a pug's face resembles that of a clinched fist.

During the Victorian period, pugs were also immensely popular, as seen by the prevalence of depictions of the breed on postcards, in paintings, and as sculptures. For many years, they continued to serve primarily as the aristocracy's pets. Both Queen Victoria and Marie Antoinette had pugs, and Queen Victoria was known to breed the breed. Marie Antoinette's pug was called Mops. In the early 1800s, they underwent the process of becoming standardized as a breed. When the English took control of the Chinese Imperial Palace in the year 1860, they found numerous pugs there and immediately started breeding them in England in an effort to enhance the breed.

Pugs did not arrive in the United States until a short time after the end of the Civil War. In 1885, the breed was given official recognition by the American Kennel Club. The Pug Dog Club of America was established in the 1930s and was later recognized by the American Kennel Club (AKC). Prior to this time, pug ownership and breeding were at an all-time high.

Left: Pug owners like dressing their dogs up! During the 9th Annual Pug Parade, which took place on February 25, 2006 in Bradenton, Florida, a pug that was dressed up like Yoda from the film Star Wars walked down the runway. Mushu, a well-trained pug, played the role of Frank, a talking pug-like extraterrestrial, in the first two films of the Men in Black film and television series. Frank was represented by an alien. During the premiere of "Men in Black 2," which took place in Los Angeles, California, he was shown here at the Mann's Village and Bruin Theaters.

Fun Facts

The American Kennel Club (AKC) cites a narrative in which a pug is said to have saved the life of the Prince of Orange by barking a warning before Spanish forces attacked, which led to the pug being the official symbol of Holland's royal House of Orange.

According to a second urban legend, some pugs were highly valued in Chinese society due to the fact that the wrinkles on their faces resembled characters in the Chinese language that denoted good fortune.

The collective noun for a bunch of pugs is "grumble."

It should come as no surprise that the adorable faces of pugs have been captured on film. There's Frank from "Men in Black," Otis from "The Adventures of Milo and Otis," and Percy from "Pocahontas." In recent years, a number of pugs have achieved insta-fame on the photo-sharing platform Instagram. There is no contest: Doug the Pug is by far the most well-liked of the lot. The famous dog has more than 13 million social followers, and because of this, he is friends with celebrities like Joe Jonas and Shakira. Doug won a People's Choice Award for Animal Star in 2019, which he received this year.

Pug owners and aficionados are just as eccentric and lovable as the breed itself. They often dress up their dogs in costumes and hold get-togethers as well as parades centered around the pug.

TH END

www.ingramcontent.com/pod-product-compliance
Lightning Source LLC
Chambersburg PA
CBHW071217260726
48653CB00041B/890